Stories On Stone

Rock Art: Images from the Ancient Ones

Jennifer Owings Dewey

Little, Brown and Company
Boston   New York   Toronto   London

To Bud Whiteford,
with gratitude for his assistance
and enthusiastic support

First Edition

Library of Congress Cataloging-in-Publication Data
Dewey, Jennifer.
    Stories on stone : rock art : images from the ancient ones /
Jennifer Owings Dewey. — 1st ed.
        p.   cm.
    ISBN 0-316-18211-7
    1. Pueblo Indians — Antiquities — Juvenile literature.
2. Petroglyphs — Southwest, New — Juvenile literature. 3. Rock
paintings — Southwest, New — Juvenile literature. 4. Indians of North
America — Southwest, New — Antiquities — Juvenile literature.
5. Southwest, New — Antiquities — Juvenile literature. [1. Pueblo
Indians — Antiquities. 2. Rock paintings. 3. Indians of North
America — Southwest, New — Antiquities. 4. Southwest, New —
Antiquities.] I. Title.
E99.P9D38 1996
979'.01 — dc20   94-3510

10 9 8 7 6 5 4 3 2 1

NIL

Published simultaneously in Canada
by Little, Brown & Company (Canada) Limited

Printed in Italy

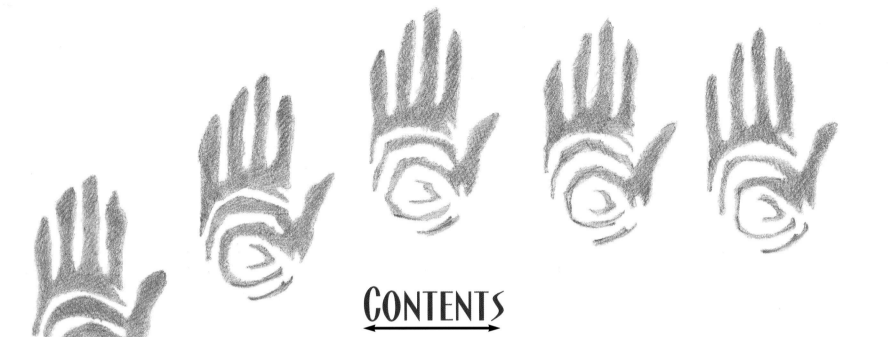

Contents

↔

THE PEOPLE, WHO WERE THEY?

When I was a child, growing up in the Southwest, my family took car trips. We often went in search of rock art — ancient images on stone that are found throughout the region.

One hot July day, my parents, brother, and I walked single file along a ridge in the Mimbres Valley, a rock art site in southern New Mexico. The stone under our feet was volcanic — black boulders tumbled on a steep slope. Pecked into the rock surfaces were hundreds, if not thousands, of images. There were pictures of birds, snakes, deer, mountain sheep, and suns.

Some of the figures were eight feet tall. Others were six feet high, or three. Some measured only inches. To my eyes, each one was magical and strange.

A picture of a turtle caught my eye. I tried to imagine the person who had created it. I had been reading and studying all I could about rock art. And although little is known of the people who chipped out the rock images in the Mimbres Valley, since they left few traces of their lives behind, I knew enough to help my imagination along.

I knew that the turtle's creator might have lived in the valley two thousand years before my visit there. I decided the artist was a man — thin, with long black hair hanging loose. I pictured him pecking at the black volcanic rock with a hard stone, one he had used again and again.

I imagined the man was a husband and father, with a wife and children waiting for him in a grove of cottonwoods not far off. There, too, would be the other members of his clan. Many clans — bands of people who lived and traveled together — took their names from animals. Perhaps this clan had named itself after the turtle.

I imagined that the man was making the turtle to thank the spirits for good luck in hunting — or perhaps to ask for better luck in the next hunt.

Once finished with his work, the man would rejoin his family and clan members in the trees. He would know that anyone passing would see the turtle and understand what it meant.

On another family trip, we visited Nine Mile Canyon, a remote rock art site in southern Utah. We hiked deep into the canyon, where I saw images painted on sandstone walls. Some of the pictures were of kachinas, spirits that are half human, half god. The kachina figures were ten feet tall, with boxy bodies and shields. Their faces were covered by masks decorated with zigzags and circles.

I also saw painted images of antelope, bird tracks, and mountain sheep, as well as handprints — many of which fit my own ten-year-old hands. Later I learned that handprints are universal. They exist on walls and stone all around the world.

Rock art occurs wherever people once lived or camped. These marks on stone say, "We were here. We traveled this way." These pictures are a mysterious but readable record of human history.

Before the advent of written language, people lived as nomads. They traveled in small bands and tribes, following seasonal cycles. They wintered in caves and summered in temporary camps. To eat, they hunted, trapped small game, and gathered wild food.

Until the end of the last Ice Age, no humans yet roamed the wilderness of what is now North America. But when the ice receded, it exposed a land bridge from northern Asia to North America, and bands of nomads migrated across it. They were the true discoverers of America.

Small scattered bands trekked across forested plains and grassy prairies, making their way toward warmer climates than those they had left behind. Some found the southwestern region of the continent to their liking, and so they remained.

There were many tribes in the region, and each had its own language. In the beginning, these people, now called paleo-Indians, kept their nomadic way of life. Some of their descendants live as nomads today. But then an important discovery made its way north from Mexico: the art of farming. Not all tribes took up this new lifeway, but most did. They continued to hunt and trap as well, but now they no longer had to wander in search of food and shelter. They could become settled.

No one knows just when it happened, that discovery of saving seeds and planting them in the ground. We do know that early southwestern people planted corn, squash, and beans. They invented systems of ditches to carry scarce rainwater to their crops. When fields were harvested, the food was stored in stone granaries to keep it safe from rodents.

Farming tribes gathered in settlements on mesa tops and in river valleys. They built permanent dwellings — well-constructed pueblos, or towns — out of stone.

One of the most important cultures of the ancient Southwest was the Anasazi. The name means "ancient ones" or perhaps "enemies of ancient ones." No one agrees on the true meaning. Made up of many tribes, the Anasazi culture emerged about two thousand years ago.

The Anasazi were not alone in choosing a village way of life. Nor were they the first. However, they grew to be the most populous and widely dispersed of the early people who settled in the high desert and mountainous areas of the region.

Traces of the Anasazi exist all across their ancestral homelands. We can still see remains of cliff houses; kivas, or sacred rooms; granaries; and rock art.

To fathom the Anasazi, one must read the signs they left behind — their stories on stone.

Myths, Spirits, and Shooting Stars

When I was very young and just beginning my quest for knowledge of rock art, a friend of my parents, a woman artist, agreed to let me tag along on trips she took to Anasazi sites.

One day, we hiked along the edge of the Rio Grande, New Mexico's longest and biggest river. There are many rock art sites along the river, on both the east and west banks.

On that day, the two of us scrambled and crawled over huge boulders of black volcanic rock. Most of the rock surfaces had images pecked out of them.

There were stick figures, such as a child might draw. There were lizards with long claws, turkey tracks, and roadrunners with their long tails up. There were faces with bulging eyes and snakes in coils. Some of the images looked like dancers.

I was so taken with what I saw, I decided to do rock art myself. Perhaps Anasazi children had pecked pictures on stone. Why not me? I experimented and soon learned it is more difficult to make rock art than it appears.

To create images on stone, the Anasazi used resources they discovered in the landscape around them.

The word for a pecked or chipped image is *petroglyph*. The tool used to create petroglyphs is usually flint, a common kind of stone in the Southwest.

Painted images are called pictographs. To create them, the ancient ones made brushes out of yucca fibers, twigs, and animal hairs. They tied these into bundles with string made from animal gut cut into strips.

Paints were made by mixing animal blood, fat, or the whites of wild bird eggs with crushed flowers, plant roots, or minerals. Black came from charcoal or roasted graphite. Other colors were made by grinding down copper ore, which gave blues and greens, or iron oxide for reds.

It takes time and the right tools to create an image on stone. A friend who studies rock art once told me that ancient artists might ask a friend or family member to play music on a flute while the work went on. We cannot know for sure whether the musician came along for fun and distraction or for spiritual reasons. The music to work by probably served more than a single purpose.

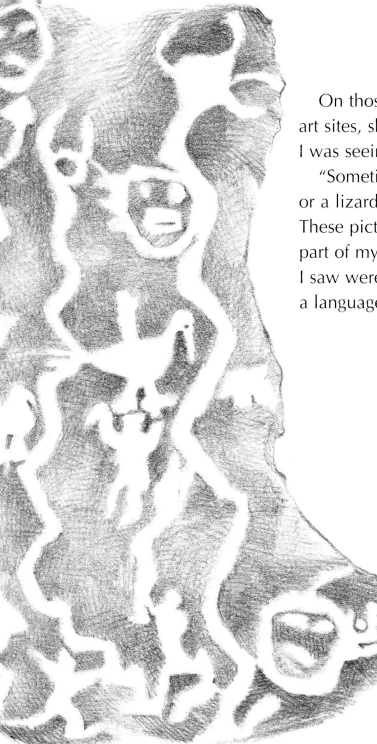

On those long-ago trips with my friend to rock art sites, she used to ask me if I understood what I was seeing.

"Sometimes," I said. I could recognize a snake or a lizard, a roadrunner with its tail in the air. These pictures were familiar to me. They were part of my experience. Yet many of the images I saw were mysterious and unfamiliar, much like a language I could not speak, read, or write.

One day, we saw an image of a mask with a long nose. "Do you know what that is?" she asked me. I did not know then and still have no certain answer.

A creature as common as a lizard becomes a different animal once it comes to exist on a rock surface. The meaning of the image was certainly wider and deeper for the maker than for me, a modern person.

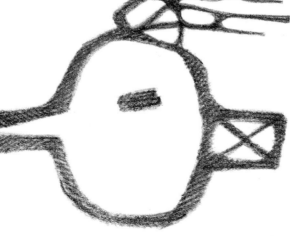

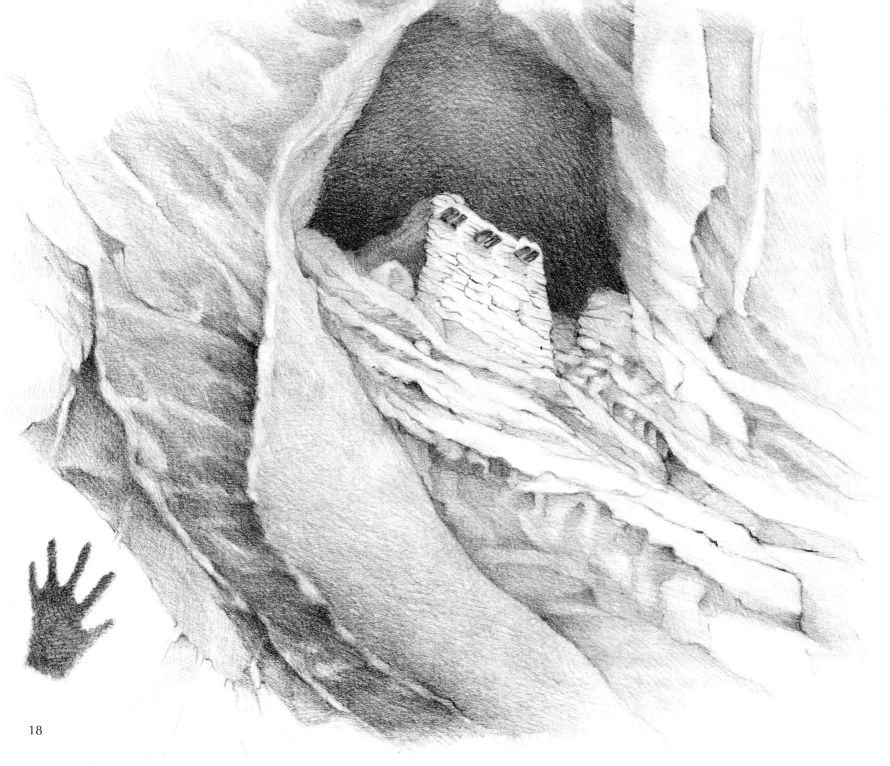

When I was still new to learning about rock art, my artist friend took me to a place where stone houses had been built on a ledge in a canyon wall. Narrow paths led to the dwellings, one hundred feet or more above the canyon floor.

The paths were so old that they cut ruts into the rock. As we climbed, I found a tiny turquoise bead and many bits of broken pottery. Then I saw a drawing of a humpbacked flute player.

"What is that?" I asked.

"Kokopelli," she told me. "A magic man, a spirit being. To some, because he has a bent back, he is especially wise. To others, he is a trickster — someone who makes mischief."

I puzzled over what she said to me. In my culture, someone with a bent back was not considered wise or special.

Since that time, I have come to know that Kokopelli means different things to different people at various times. Though his true meaning may remain unrevealed, I knew when I saw him that he had magic powers, if not for me directly then for somebody sometime.

Since we are not them, the Anasazi, we can only imagine what they felt as they pecked or painted their stories on stone.

Those who study rock art and attempt to translate the past say that many different sorts of people created pictographs and petroglyphs. Among them were medicine men and women, who possessed holy powers. These people were able to bridge the gap between the world of spirits and that of everyday. They made many of the images we see today.

Other, less holy, more ordinary people
were given the task of recording the daily life
of the pueblo, or town. Sometimes these people
made pictures on stones to describe the birth
of a new baby, the death of a parent, or the arri-
val of a swarm of insects. They also made images
of celestial events, such as a solar eclipse or
a meteor shower.

When I was twelve, I came upon the image of a shooting star chipped into the surface of a darkly colored rock. The picture was small, less than a foot across. People had been in that place. One of them saw a shooting star and was moved to record the experience on stone.

Many reasons drove people to make rock art. From the time the first human beings banged one rock on another, rock art has created visual connections. The images link the commonplace with the mysterious. Rock art is concerned with spirits, fear, and hope. These ancient marks on stone are maps of the human heart, mind, and imagination.

THE PEOPLE TODAY

The Anasazi have not vanished, even though their many tribes and towns are buried in dust from centuries of wind blowing across the land.

They remain in a transformed way. The Pueblo people are the modern descendants of the ancient Anasazi bands who roamed, hunted, trapped, and finally settled into a farming way of life.

The Pueblo people live the old way, in harmony with the earth and the seasons. They continue to make art, including images on stone.

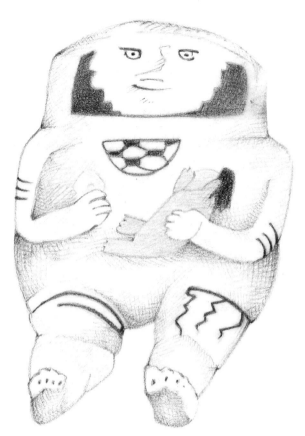

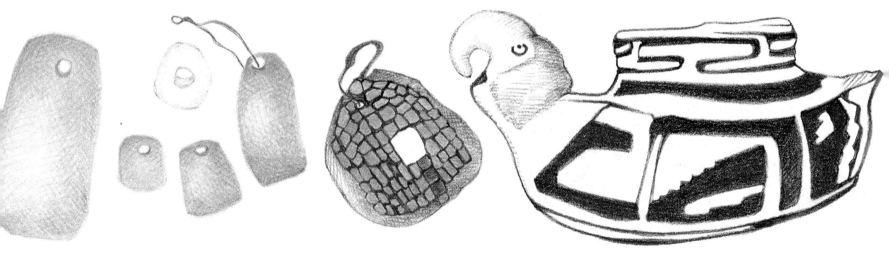

The Pueblo people are secretive and protective of their sacred works, their pictographs and petroglyphs. A friend of mine once asked a Taos Pueblo man who made the pictures on stone along the Rio Grande.

"Witches," he said, grinning.

The Pueblo people are aware of the mysterious and spiritual side of life. Even though rock art is hard to fully comprehend, because so little evidence is left to us, we still have our power to dream and imagine what these images mean now and what they once meant to those who made them.

29

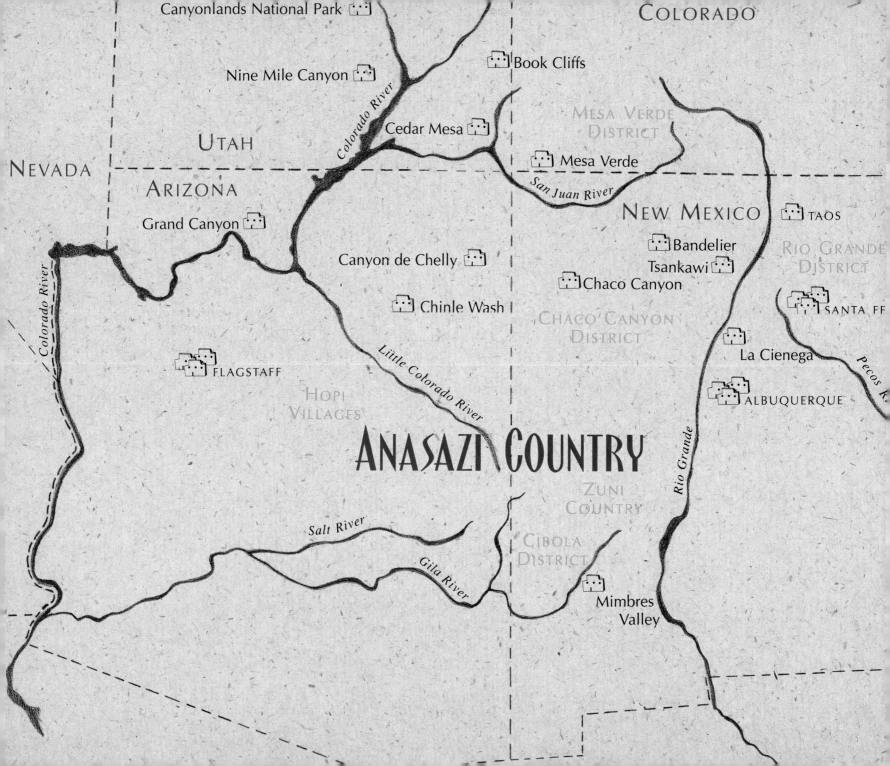

LEGEND

STATES

DISTRICTS

CITIES & TOWNS

Sites

Author's Note

⟷

Whenever you encounter a remnant of an ancient culture —
a picture on a rock, the ruins of a dwelling, or a huge pyramid —
remember how old it is. Be one of those people who look at the
remains of the past with curiosity, respect, and no desire to do harm.
Listen to the story these ancient creations tell you — and let the
story be heard by the next person who comes along.